CRYSTALS
AND
CRYSTAL GARDENS
YOU CAN GROW

CRYSTALS

AND
CRYSTAL GARDENS
YOU CAN GROW

BY JEAN STANGL

Franklin Watts
New York ❖ London ❖ Toronto ❖ Sydney
A First Book

Library of Congress Cataloging-in-Publication Data

Stangl, Jean.
Crystals and crystal gardens you can grow/by Jean Stangl.
p. cm.—(A First book)
Includes bibliographical references.
Summary: Provides scientific explanations for the formation of
crystals, tips for growing them, and instructions for experiments.
ISBN 0-531-10889-9
1. Crystals—Juvenile literature. 2. Crystals—Growth—Juvenile
literature. [1. Crystals—Experiments. 2. Experiments.]
I. Title. II. Title: Crystal gardens you can grow. III. Series.
QD921.S66   1990
548'.5'078—dc20   89-38999 CIP AC

For Kenna,
who likes to grow
crystal gardens

CONTENTS

Crystal Formations
11

Crystals You Can Grow
30

Magic Crystal Gardens
46

How Does Your Crystal Garden Grow?
58

For Further Reading 61
Index 62

CRYSTALS
AND
CRYSTAL GARDENS
YOU CAN GROW

Common table salt magnified to show its cubelike structure

CRYSTAL
FORMATIONS

Every day you see many different crystals. You probably even eat some!

Did you eat any salt or sugar today? If so, then you ate some crystals, for both salt and sugar are crystals.

A grain of salt is a tiny cubelike crystal. Place a few grains of salt on a piece of black paper. Look at the salt grains with a magnifying glass. What do you see? Place a few grains of sugar on the paper. Do they look the same as the salt crystals? No, because the sugar crystals have a different shape.

Matter is everything that makes up the world, and all matter is made up of **atoms,** or arrangements of atoms called **molecules.** (An atom is the basic unit of matter, and molecules are similar or different atoms chemically bound together.) All matter comes in one of three forms—solid, liquid, or gas. Water can take all three of these forms. It can be liquid, like the water you drink; gas, like steam vapor from boiling water; or solid, as when it is placed in the freezer until it becomes ice.

A crystal is a solid form of a substance; in it, the atoms or molecules are arranged in an orderly pattern that is repeated over and over again throughout the whole crystal. The atoms are like tiny building blocks, and the crystal is made up of millions of atoms that fit together in their own special pattern to form that crystal.

Salt crystals are shaped like cubes. In other crystals, the atoms or groups of atoms are arranged in different shapes. Most scientists believe there are seven types of crystals.

Most nonliving substances are made up of crystals. Salt, sugar, sand, diamonds, and snowflakes are all made up of crystals. However, early in history, scientists thought that only ice and the clear, colorless mineral called rock quartz were crystals. After much research and many experiments, they discovered that crystals can be found in materials that are colored or colorless, hard or soft enough to be cut with a knife, and in some substances that can be melted,

The Seven Types of Crystals

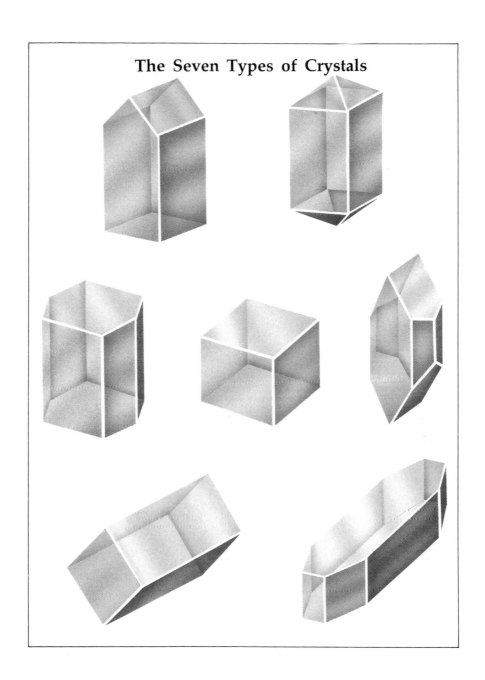

Snowflakes are the miniwonders of nature,
with their complexity and beauty.

such as gold. When heated to a certain point, gold becomes a liquid. But one thing all crystals have in common is that they have a definite shape. They also have flat surfaces, called **faces.** Where two or more of these faces meet, you will find angles (or edges or corners).

This false-color photo of table salt shows the crystal's many faces.

When you look at grains of salt with your magnifying glass, some may not appear to be perfect cubes. The reason for this is that some crystals do not form under ideal conditions, that is, undisturbed by other minerals that are starting to **crystallize** (become crystals). Some of the crystals might also appear to be chipped or nicked from rubbing against each other.

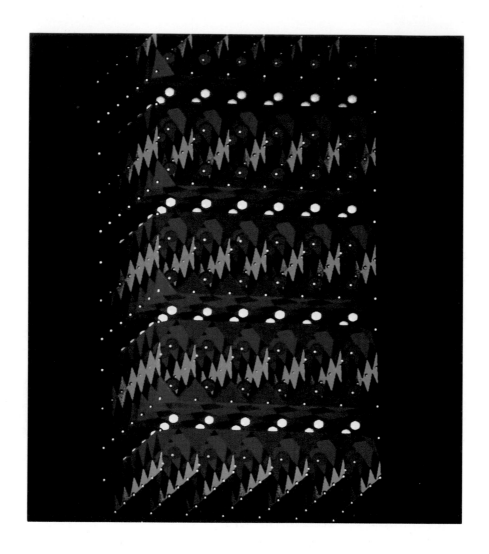

Crystallographers study many different types of crystals. Here is a computer graphic of a molecule of a high-temperature superconductor, showing the material's crystal structure.

Crystallography is the study of crystals, and a **crystallographer** is a scientist who studies the arrangement of the atoms that make up crystals.

This book will help you begin to understand crystals and will tell you where you can find different types of crystals. Before you are through, you will also know how to make crystals and grow crystal "gardens."

WHERE TO FIND CRYSTALS

Most minerals and rocks are made up of crystals. **Minerals** are nonliving chemical substances that are found in nature. The minerals that make up rocks, sand, and gravel provide us with familiar examples of crystals. The minerals sulfur, copper, and silver, and the graphite used in pencils, are sometimes found as naturally occurring crystals.

Rocks are usually made up of two or more kinds of minerals. Quartz, the common mineral found in many types of rocks, is often called *rock crystal*. Quartz crystals may be transparent or colored, but they are always six-sided (as long as their growth is not interfered with by that of other crystals).

The sea is a giant storehouse of minerals. Dried-up lakes and oceans have deposited layers and layers

*Quartz, or rock crystal, is
a common mineral found in rock.
It can be quite dazzling to
the eye and is always six-sided.*

of minerals. About one-third of the world's salt, a mineral, is harvested from the ocean.

Coal is an example of a rock that is not made up of minerals. It is formed from plants that died many millions of years ago. Sugar is a crystal, but it is not a mineral. Sugar comes from plants, either sugarcane or sugar beets.

Look for rocks in your yard, the park, empty lots, or riverbeds. You can find white, black, and other colors of crystals in sand and gravel. The jagged edge of a freshly broken rock or a shiny rock soaked in water will provide some interesting discoveries.

Sand often contains crystals of many different colors, sizes, and shapes. This sand is from a beach in Saskatchewan.

*Petrified wood from the Petrified Forest
National Park in Arizona*

Shale, marble, slate, granite, and petrified wood contain crystals that can be found with your magnifying glass. If you can't find any rocks with crystals, collections of rocks can be seen in museums, gem shows, county fairs, and hobby shops.

A geode looks like an ugly brown rock. But when it is split open, you can see that its hollow center is surrounded by beautiful black, purple, and colorless crystals. Geodes average from 2 to 6 inches (5 to 15 cm) in diameter. They can be found in the southwestern United States and Mexico, and also in other parts of the world. But they are not easy to find. If you know any rock hounds (rock collectors), ask them to show you some from their collection.

A geode split open to show its surprising insides

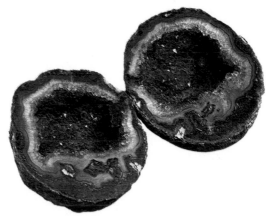

Crystals are also found in precious gems such as diamonds and rubies, and in gold, iron, copper, and other metals.

Many people think glass is made up of crystals because it is clear and sparkling. However, it is not; its atoms are not arranged in an orderly pattern. Glass can be molded into many forms, but it will not take a definite shape of its own. Most glass is made from melted quartz sand that is cooled too rapidly for its atoms and molecules to arrange themselves into an orderly pattern.

*Crystals of precious gems and even
some metals can be fascinating to look at
and are often on display in museums.*

Top row: amethyst, calcite, mita-torberrite, elbaite tourmaline. Bottom row: Copper, galena, emerald, and aquamarine.

*Snowflakes come in an astonishing array
of designs. In fact, it is believed that
no two snowflakes are exactly alike.*

A snowflake is a crystal that forms from a gas—
water vapor. If we magnified an average snowflake,
we might see that it consists of several six-sided crystals. When the tiny snow crystals fall to earth during
a snowfall, they bump into each other, stick together,
and form the lacy mass we see as a snowflake.

Break an ice cube or the end off an icicle. Examine the irregular surface with your magnifying glass. Can you see the crystals? On a cold morning, you may find frost (ice crystals) on grass, trees, or a window pane.

Icicles on a tree in winter

Frost on a star thistle flower and a window pane

Many types of crystals have been produced by scientists to make artificial gems, such as synthetic, or manufactured, rubies or diamonds. Artificial crystals have also been produced for use in transistors in radios, pacemakers (devices to regulate heartbeat), and computers.

Crystals are all around us, but many are too small to be seen with the naked eye. Use your magnifying glass to examine the world around you, and you will be surprised at how many beautiful crystals you will find.

TIPS FOR EXPERIMENTERS

Learning about crystals can be fun and exciting. By growing crystals and crystal gardens, you will be able to observe, experiment, and make interesting discoveries, just as scientists do.

Most of the materials used in the experiments described in this book are ordinary things you can find in the kitchen or elsewhere around the house. (Be sure, though, to ask your parents' permission to use these items.) A good magnifying glass is an important tool that will help you to examine your crystals more closely.

What you will need

Spoons

Plastic
Drinking
Cups

Margarine Container

Pie Plate

Measuring Cup

Tablespoon

BASIC UTENSILS

Old metal spoons or plastic picnic spoons
Clear plastic drinking glasses
Clean, used containers such as margarine tubs or
    disposable aluminum foil piepans
Measuring cups and spoons

BEFORE YOU START

Read through this book.
Read the directions for each experiment carefully.
Gather your materials.
Follow the directions *exactly.*
Measure carefully.
Be patient!

Note: In order to grow some crystals mentioned in this book, you will need to heat the solution. Do this *only* with adult supervision. If a stove is not available, you can use an electric frying pan.

CRYSTALS
YOU CAN GROW

Many different kinds of substances can be used to produce interesting crystals—as long as the substance you start with is made up of crystals. Sugar and salt offer good possibilities for experimenting, as they produce fascinating crystal formations. Both sugar and salt crystals can be grown in a number of different ways. The directions are easy to follow, and the experiments can be done in either the classroom or at home.

Salt crystals are cubelike, with flat sides, or faces. Sugar crystals are oblong in form and beveled (slanted) sharply at either end. Alum, another interesting crystal, is a bitter white powder (mineral) that

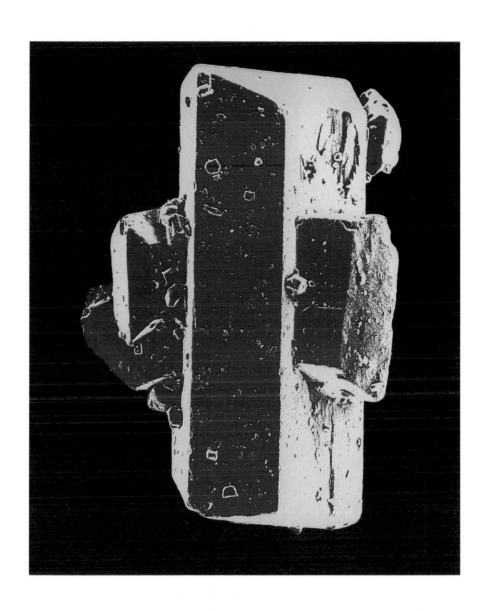

*A sugar crystal
(notice its oblong form).*

Alum crystals (the white ones are pure, the others colored with a dye).

is used in baking powder. Alum crystals have eight triangular faces.

The easiest way to grow crystals is from a solution. A solid, such as salt or sugar, dissolved in water makes the right kind of solution. A liquid dissolved in a liquid (i.e., ammonia in water) also makes the right kind of solution. Gas, such as carbon dioxide, in a liquid, makes the solution (carbonated) soda; it is the CO_2 that fizzes in your drink. In the following projects, you will grow crystals in solutions made by dissolving solids in liquids or liquids in liquids.

SATURATED AND
SUPERSATURATED SOLUTIONS

WHAT YOU NEED

¹/₂ cup of cold water	a small pan
1 cup of sugar	the use of a stove (Use
a teaspoon	the stove only in the
a stirring spoon	presence of an adult.)

WHAT YOU DO

Add a teaspoon of sugar to the cup of water and stir until dissolved. Then continue to add sugar, one teaspoonful at a time, until no more will dissolve. Pour this solution into the pan. Place the pan on a stove and warm slowly over low heat, until the solution is hot but not boiling. With a potholder, remove the pan from the stove. Carefully (the pan is hot) add 4 teaspoons of sugar and stir.

When a solution contains as much dissolved material as it can hold at that temperature, it is said to be **saturated.** The cold water was saturated with sugar. By heating the solution, however, you changed the properties of the water, and the mixture was no longer a saturated solution. Thus, more sugar could be dissolved in it. If, after saturating your solution at a high temperature, it is allowed to cool, the solution will become **supersaturated.**

CRYSTALS ON A PENCIL

WHAT YOU NEED

2 tablespoons of rock salt
   (found in the super-
   market near table salt;
   usually used in making
   ice cream)
1 cup of hot tap water
a spoon for stirring
a piece of string
a pencil

WHAT YOU DO

Add the 2 tablespoons of rock salt to the cup of hot water. Stir until dissolved.

Tie a piece of string around the pencil. Place the pencil across the top of the cup, with the string dangling in the salt water. Place the experiment in a sunny place.

Check the experiment often, but don't expect results for about twenty-four hours. Be sure to check the underside of the pencil!

Note: You may want to try this experiment using a piece of yarn or a thin rope or cord instead of the string.

Crystals on a Pencil

What you will need:

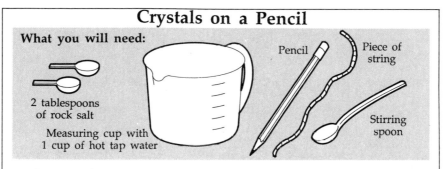

Pencil

Piece of string

2 tablespoons of rock salt

Measuring cup with 1 cup of hot tap water

Stirring spoon

What you do:

Add 2 tablespoons of rock salt to the tap water.
Stir until dissolved.
Tie a piece of string around the pencil.

Place the pencil across the top of the cup with the string hanging in the salt water.

Place the experiment in the sun.

What do you see ?

GOOD-TO-EAT CRYSTALS

WHAT YOU NEED
1½ cups of sugar
½ cup of boiling water
   (Ask an adult for
   help in handling
   the boiling water.)
a spoon for stirring
an empty cup
food coloring
a clean piece of string
a pencil
a clean paper clip

WHAT YOU DO
Bring the water to a boil in a pan. With a potholder, remove the pan from the heat. Add the sugar to the boiling water and stir until dissolved. Pour the solution into a cup. (A Pyrex measuring cup works well.) Stir in 3 drops of food coloring. Tie one end of a piece of string around the center of the pencil. Tie the other end to the paper clip. Place the pencil across the top of the cup so that the string and paper clip dangle in the water. Set the cup aside for a few days, but check it daily. Don't touch or shake!

    Your colorful sugar crystals can now be eaten!

SPECIAL CRYSTALS

WHAT YOU NEED
$\frac{1}{2}$ cup of water
an aluminum foil piepan
a cooking pan
a spoon for stirring
salt
the use of a stove
   (Check with an
   adult before
   using the stove.)

WHAT YOU DO
Heat the water in the pan until almost boiling. Carefully pour the hot water into the foil pan. Add the salt, a little at a time. Stir well. Dissolve as much salt as possible in the water. Allow the solution to cool. It will then be supersaturated. It cannot hold any more salt.

    Place the pan in a safe spot, where it will not be disturbed. Check frequently.

    The slower the water evaporates, the larger the crystals you will see.

WALNUT-SHAPED CRYSTALS

WHAT YOU NEED
1 ounce of alum
   (can be purchased
   at the supermarket
   in the spice section)
$\frac{1}{2}$ cup of warm water
nylon thread
an empty plastic cup
a spoon for stirring
a pencil

WHAT YOU DO
Slowly add the alum to the warm water. Stir in all that the water will absorb. Let it sit overnight. The next day, pour off the water into the empty cup. A few solid pieces of alum will remain in the first cup. Wrap a piece of nylon thread around the largest solid piece. Place the pencil across the cup with the liquid. Tie the thread to the pencil so that the solid formation dangles in the alum water. Check your experiment twice a day. What do you see?

MASS OF CRYSTALS

WHAT YOU NEED
2 cups of sugar
1 cup of water
a pint jar
a small pan
a spoon for stirring
an old towel
the use of a stove
  (Ask an adult
  to help you use
  the stove.)

WHAT YOU DO
Pour the water into the pan and heat until almost boiling. Carefully remove the pan from the stove. Stir in the sugar, a half a cup at a time, until no more will dissolve. Rinse the jar with hot tap water. Pour the sugar solution into the jar. Wrap the towel around the jar so the solution will cool slowly. Place the jar where it will not be disturbed for a few days. Masses of crystals should form at the top and bottom of the jar, and a few along the sides.

FLOATING CRYSTALS

WHAT YOU NEED
2 cups of sugar
$\frac{1}{2}$ tsp. of unflavored gelatine
a small pan
a pint jar
a spoon for stirring
an old towel
the use of a stove (Ask an adult for help)

WHAT YOU DO
Pour the water into the pan. Stir in the gelatine. Heat to almost boiling. When the gelatine has gone into solution (dissolved), remove the pan from the stove. Let the solution cool for five minutes. Then stir in the sugar, a half a cup at a time, until no more will dissolve. Let it cool for five minutes. Rinse the jar with hot tap water. Pour the supersaturated solution into the jar. Wrap the towel around the jar so the solution will cool slowly. Place the jar where it will not be disturbed. Remove the towel after the jar is cool and wait for a few days. What do you see?

Sparkling, clear crystals will appear suspended (floating) through the gelatine. If possible, let the crystals continue to grow for several weeks, even several months, for large, well-formed specimens.

SODA CRYSTALS

WHAT YOU NEED
A clear plastic drinking cup
hot tap water
a measuring (tea)spoon
a spoon for stirring
washing soda
      (a laundry product,
      such as Borax,
      found in the laundry
      soaps section of
      the supermarket)

WHAT YOU DO
Fill the glass half full with hot tap water. Stir in the washing soda, one teaspoon at a time, until no more will dissolve. Set the glass aside for a day or two. What do you see?

CRYSTAL PILLARS

WHAT YOU NEED

two pint jars
a jar lid
a strip of old towel
   1 inch (2.5 cm) wide
   by 18 inches (46 cm)
   long
a measuring cup
a measuring (table)spoon

a stirring spoon
hot tap water
a tray or cookie sheet
10 tbs. of washing soda
   (can be found in the
   laundry products
   section of a super-
   market)

WHAT YOU DO

Rinse the jars with hot tap water. Pour one and a half cups of hot tap water into each jar. Add 5 tablespoons of washing soda to each jar. Stir until dissolved. Place the jars on a tray. Place the lid between them. Drop one end of the towel into each jar and let the middle of the cloth hang over the lid. Wait a few days. What do you see?

As the water and soda solution from the jars moves along the towel, it drips down in the middle, collecting in the jar lid. As it drips, the water evaporates, and the soda is left in a hard pillar. If you wait long enough, the pillars should grow up from the lid and down from the towel until they meet in the middle, forming a crystal column.

Crystal Pillars

What you need:

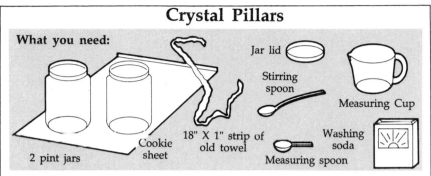

Jar lid

Stirring spoon

Measuring Cup

18" X 1" strip of old towel

Washing soda

2 pint jars

Cookie sheet

Measuring spoon

What you do:

Rinse jars in hot water and pour one and a half cups of tap water into each jar. Add 3 tablespoons of washing soda to each jar and stir until dissolved.

Place the jars on the cookie sheet with the lid between them. Then drop one end of the towel into each jar and let the middle of the cloth hang over the lid and wait overnight.

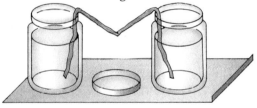

What do you see?

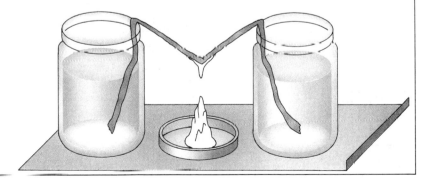

Above: Stalactites in Mitchell Caverns, in the East Mojave National Scenic Area of California, provide a spectacular sight. Right: This stalagmite is seen through a special filter, allowing us to enjoy its complexities and colors.

This is the way that columns called *stalagmites* (the ones that grow up from the floor) are formed in caves. (*Stalactites* are deposits that hang from the roof or sides of a cave or cavern.) Water, carrying lime from limestone rocks, slowly drips from the ceiling. As the water evaporates into the air, it leaves behind the lime, which forms pillars. The buildup takes many hundreds of years.

MAGIC
CRYSTAL GARDENS

You can grow crystal gardens by pouring a solution over objects in a pan or bowl. Tiny, fluffy crystals begin to grow one upon the other.

When you grow, your body is growing from the inside. Your body uses the nourishment provided by the food you eat to grow. Crystals grow from the outside. The crystals you can see growing in these gardens grow when the right kinds of atoms or molecules reach the surface and fit themselves into the same pattern. Then new crystals grow on the sides and top of the original crystal formation.

Here's a few things to keep in mind as you grow your crystal gardens:

Cover your work area with plastic or newspapers.

Wipe up any solution you spill or you may have crystals growing on the table, chair, or floor!

Use a magnifying glass to carefully examine the tiny crystal formations.

Keep a record of your experiments and see which ones produce the quickest results.

KEEP AMMONIA AWAY FROM YOUR FACE, AS THE FUMES CAN IRRITATE YOUR NOSE, THROAT, AND EYES. Close the bottle as soon as you pour out the amount you need.

A BASIC SOLUTION

Here's a simple recipe for a basic solution that can be used for a number of experiments.

WHAT YOU NEED
a clear plastic drinking cup
water
liquid laundry bluing (found in the laundry products
    section of the supermarket)
table salt
household ammonia
measuring spoons
a spoon for stirring

WHAT YOU DO

Into the cup, measure 3 tablespoons of water, 3 tablespoons of bluing, and 3 tablespoons of salt. Mix
everything together, stirring slowly. Then carefully
add 1 tablespoon of ammonia and mix well (see
page 50).

Select one or all of the following experiments,
collecting the necessary materials and placing them
in containers. Large, clean margarine tubs or other
plastic bowls or aluminum piepans are good containers. Stir the "basic solution" mixture often as you
spoon it—don't pour it—over the materials. Allow
only a small amount of liquid to remain in the bottom
of the container. You should have enough solution to
do all six projects. Here, now, are the experiments.

1. *Rock and Charcoal Garden*. You will need rocks, a
piece of coal or charcoal briquette, and a container.
Into the container, place assorted rocks and the small
piece of coal or a broken charcoal briquette. Slowly
spoon on the basic solution. Wait about twenty-four
hours for good results. What do you see?

2. *Paper Towel Garden*. You will need a container and
two paper towels. Place a folded paper towel in the
container. Crush the second paper towel and place
it on top of the folded one. Slowly spoon the ba-

sic solution onto the crushed paper towel. What do you see?

3. *Aluminum Foil Garden.* You will need a 10-inch × 10-inch (25 cm × 25 cm) piece of aluminum foil, a container, and four wooden toothpicks. Lightly crush the piece of aluminum foil and place it in the container. Lay the toothpicks across the foil. Slowly spoon the basic solution over the materials. What do you see? Crystals should begin to form soon.

4. *Porous Rock Garden.* You will need several types of porous rocks and a measuring spoon. Porous rocks are sandstones or volcanic rocks such as lava, pumice, or others that have small holes, or pores, that allow liquid to pass through. This type of rock can sometimes be found in mountain or desert areas, or along riverbeds. Pumice stones are used for smoothing rough skin and are sold in drug or cosmetic stores. Stores that carry barbecue equipment sell small bags of lava rocks that are used on the bottom of grills.

Place the rocks in the container. Cover the rocks with water and let them soak overnight. The next day, pour off the water and sprinkle a tablespoon of salt over the rocks. Slowly spoon on the basic solution. What do you see?

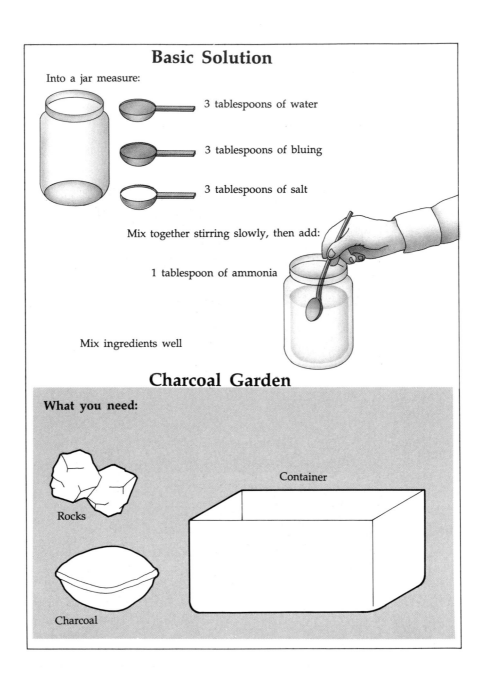

Basic Solution

Into a jar measure:

3 tablespoons of water

3 tablespoons of bluing

3 tablespoons of salt

Mix together stirring slowly, then add:

1 tablespoon of ammonia

Mix ingredients well

Charcoal Garden

What you need:

Rocks

Charcoal

Container

What you do:

Place rocks and a small piece of a broken
  charcoal briquette into the container. Slowly
  spoon on the basic solution. Wait 24 hours.

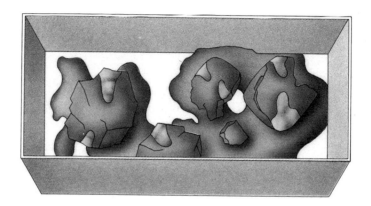

What do you see?

5. *Sponge Garden.* You will need an assortment of sponges. You can use any clean sponges—plastic sponges (the kind used for cleaning chores), florist sponges (used for flower arranging), or true sea sponges (the kind harvested from the ocean and often used as shower sponges, makeup sponges, and for washing cars); a container; a spoon for stirring.

Tear the sponges into chunks and place these in a container. Slowly spoon the basic solution over the sponges. For best results, let the experiment set for forty-eight hours. What do you see?

6. *A Garden of Odds and Ends.* You will need a styrofoam cup, an empty margarine tub, and assorted small materials such as a marble, nail, wooden spool, piece of tree bark, dry leaf, rubber band, or piece of plastic. You will also need a spoon for stirring.

Place all the items in the cup. Slowly spoon the basic solution over the materials. Place the cup in the margarine tub. You should have results in minutes. Crystals should form on the inside of the cup and spread over the top.

SUPER CRYSTAL GARDEN

Fill a large plastic or aluminum foil pan with all the materials listed in the six experiments above. Then add your own favorite items. Double the basic solution recipe and slowly spoon it over your collection of materials. What do you see?

SURPRISE GARDEN

You will need a large, clean margarine tub, warm water, salt, vinegar, porous rocks (see *Porous Rock Garden*, above), measuring spoons, and a stirring spoon. Fill the margarine tub half full with warm water. Add the salt, one teaspoon at a time. Stir until well dissolved. You can "feel" with the stirring spoon when most of the salt is dissolved. Stir in one teaspoon of vinegar. Place the rocks in the solution. Check in a few hours for results. Salt crystals should develop on your rocks.

BRICK CASTLE

You will need broken pieces of a building brick or clay flower pot, a deep bowl or other container, water, liquid laundry bluing, household ammonia, salt, food coloring, a clear plastic drinking cup, a measuring spoon, and a spoon for stirring.

Place the broken pieces of the brick in the bowl. Cover with water and soak until the brick pieces are thoroughly wet. Pour off the water and arrange the pieces in a castlelike pile in the container. Into the cup, measure and mix 4 tablespoons of water, 4 tablespoons of liquid laundry bluing, and 4 tablespoons of household ammonia. Pour the solution over the wet rocks, making sure they are all dampened. Now sprinkle 4 tablespoons of salt over the chunks of brick, covering them evenly.

Within a few hours, tiny "snowflakes" should appear on the bricks. To give color to your garden, sprinkle on a few drops of various shades of food coloring. After about two days, measure and mix in a clean plastic cup 2 tablespoons of water and 2 tablespoons of ammonia. Pour this mixture into the dish.

Your garden should grow for several weeks. What do you see?

MYSTERY GARDEN

This is a three-day experiment. You will need a large, clean, plastic margarine container, water, broken pieces of coal or charcoal, pieces from a broken clay flowerpot, bits of sea sponges, a tablespoon, salt, liquid laundry bluing, household ammonia, and a clear plastic drinking cup.

Soak for fifteen minutes the pieces of coal or charcoal, the flowerpot pieces, and the sponge in the margarine tub filled with water. Pour off the water.

Mystery Garden

What you need:

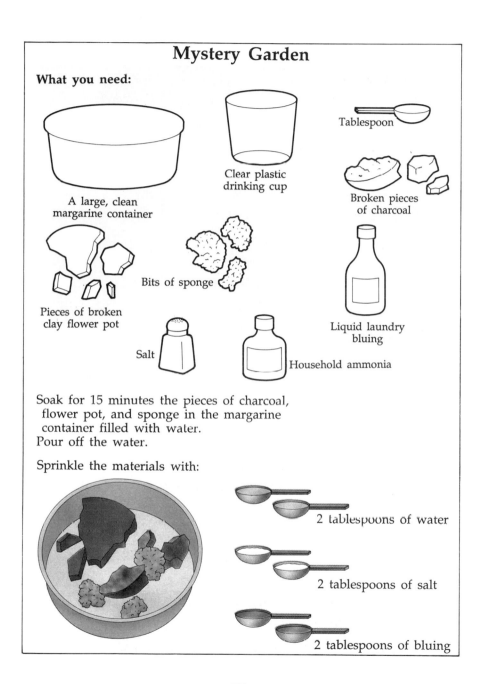

A large, clean margarine container

Clear plastic drinking cup

Tablespoon

Broken pieces of charcoal

Pieces of broken clay flower pot

Bits of sponge

Liquid laundry bluing

Salt

Household ammonia

Soak for 15 minutes the pieces of charcoal, flower pot, and sponge in the margarine container filled with water.
Pour off the water.

Sprinkle the materials with:

2 tablespoons of water

2 tablespoons of salt

2 tablespoons of bluing

On the second day, sprinkle
2 more tablespoons
of salt over the materials.

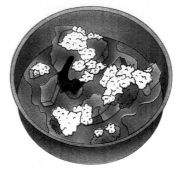

On the third day, measure into the cup:

2 tablespoons of salt

2 tablespoons of water

2 tablespoons of bluing

2 tablespoons of ammonia

Mix well and pour the solution into the bottom
of the container, not on the crystals.

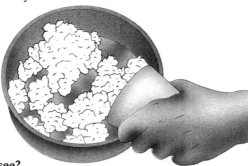

What do you see?

Sprinkle the wet materials with 2 tablespoons of water, then with 2 tablespoons of salt, and then with 2 tablespoons of bluing.

On the second day, sprinkle 2 more tablespoons of salt over the materials. On the third day, measure into the cup 2 tablespoons of salt, 2 tablespoons of water, 2 tablespoons of bluing, and 2 tablespoons of ammonia. Mix well and pour the solution into the *bottom* of the container (not on the crystals). What do you see?

When your garden seems to stop growing, mix up a fresh batch of solution (see third day) and carefully spoon it onto the materials. New crystals will form, and your garden should last for several months.

Sprinkling food coloring over the crystals should produce some interesting surprises. Also try experimenting with drops of bluing, fruit juice (grape, cherry, or cranberry), and watercolors (paints).

HOW DOES YOUR CRYSTAL GARDEN GROW?

Think about your observations. Do you think you were actually *growing* crystal gardens?

All the materials you used for the experiments in this book were nonliving. Minerals can change, but only living things—plants and animals—actually grow. They take in food and convert it into building materials that are used for growth. Did your crystal gardens do this?

Then how did the crystals form? Why did they keep getting bigger?

Salt is a mineral made up of tiny crystals.

Bluing is a liquid containing tiny bits of blue powder.

Ammonia is a colorless gas that dissolves in water. Household ammonia is a water solution of this gas.

We say that you "grew" a crystal garden, but here's what really happened. After the salt dissolved in the water, the salty water was absorbed by, or flowed into, the porous materials—the rocks, the sponges, the paper. The liquid evaporated, and the mineral residue (salt) recrystallized around the blue powder bits. Liquid will continue to move to the surface of the newly formed crystals, and crystals will form on top of crystals. New crystals will continue to form until all the solution evaporates.

What you saw was a process of dissolving, absorbing, evaporating, and crystallizing. Ammonia speeds up evaporation, causing the crystals to form more rapidly.

Did you see any colors in your crystals? What do you think caused them? Did the excess water in the bottom of the garden container change colors?

The colors you saw in the crystals and in the excess liquid were from the minerals in the rocks and other materials you used.

Sometimes, these gardens are called "chemical gardens," but no chemical reactions actually take place, just dissolving and recrystallization.

A PROPER ENVIRONMENT

It is important to have proper surroundings in order to produce a beautiful garden. Set your garden either indoors or in a sheltered spot outside. Place it in a shaded area where the air can circulate freely. Dry air is best. If you had poor results with your first attempt, try again.

What do you think would happen if

You left out the ammonia?
You added extra ammonia?
You left out the bluing?
You added extra bluing?
You used more salt?
You covered the garden with clear plastic wrap?

Experiment and find out. You will make some exciting discoveries, and you may find a new way to grow a crystal or a crystal garden!

FOR FURTHER READING

Berry, James. *Exploring Crystals*. New York: Crowell-Collier, 1969.

Gans, Roma. *Millions and Millions of Crystals*. New York: Crowell, 1973.

Sanders, Lenore. *The Curious World of Crystals*. New York: Prentice-Hall, 1964.

Shuttlesworth, Dorothy. *The Story of Rocks*. New York: Doubleday, 1966.

Zim, Herbert. *Diamonds*. New York: William Morrow, 1959.

————. *Rocks and Minerals*. New York: Golden Press, 1957.

————. *Quartz*. New York: William Morrow, 1981.

INDEX

*Page numbers in italics
represent illustrations.*

Alum, 30, 32
    in walnut-shaped crystals,
        38
Aluminum foil garden, 49
Amethyst, 22
Ammonia, 32, 47, 54, 57, 59
    safety in use of, 47
Aquamarine, 23
Atoms, 11–12

Bluing, 47, 48, 54, 57, 58
Brick castle crystal garden, 53

Calcite, 22
Carbon dioxide (CO_2), 32

Charcoal, 54, 57
"Chemical gardens," 59
Clay pots, 53, 54
Coal, 19, 54, 57
Colors, 59
Computers, 27
Containers, 48
Copper, 17, 21, 22
Crystal gardens, 46–47
    basic solution for, 47–49, 52
    directions for growing, 47
    environment for, 60
    types to grow, 48–49, 52–54,
        57
Crystallization, 15
Crystallographers, *16*, 17
Crystallography, 17
Crystal pillars, 42, 44, 45

Crystals, 17
    angles on, 15
    atoms and molecules in, 12
    faces of, 15
    ice, 12
    locations of, 17, 19, 20, 21, 24,
      25, 27
    materials found in, 12, 15
    process of forming, 59
    seven types of, 12, *13*
    structure of, 11, 12, 15, *16*, *18*
    synthetic, 27
Crystals on a pencil, 34

Diamonds, 12, 21
    synthetic, 27

Elbaite tournaline, 23
Emeralds, 23
Evaporation of water, 37
Experiments, 27, 29, 30–57
    material for, 27, 29
    preparation for, 29
    substances used, 30

Floating crystals, 40
Food coloring, 36, 57
Frost, 25, *26*

Galena, 22
Gases, 12
Gelatine, 40
Gems, 21, 22, 23
    synthetic, 27
Geodes, 20–21
Glass, 21
Gold, 12, 15, 21

Good-to-eat crystals, 36
Granite, 20
Graphite, 17
Growing crystals, 30, 32

Icicles, 25
Iron, 21

Limestone, 45
Liquid solutions, 32

Magnifying glass, 27, *28*, 47
Marble, 20
Mass of crystals, 39
Matter, 11–12
    three forms of, 12
Measuring, 29
Metals, 21, 22, 23
Minerals, 17
Mita-torberrite, 23
Molecules, 11–12
Mystery garden, 54, 57

Odds-and-ends crystal garden, 52

Pacemakers, 27
Paper towel garden, 48–49
Pencil experiment, 34
Petrified wood, 20
Porous rock garden, 49
Porous rocks, 49, 53

Quartz, 17, *18*

Radio crystals, 27
Record keeping, 47
Recrystallization, 59

Rock and charcoal garden, 48
Rock crystal (quartz), 17, *18*
Rock hounds, 21
Rock quartz, 17, *18*
Rock salt, 34
Rubies, 21
    synthetic, 27

Salt crystals, *10*, 12, 19, 58
    experiments with, 30, 37, 54,
      57
Sand, *19*
Saturated solutions, 33
Sea, 17, 19
Shale, 20
Silver, 17
Slate, 20
Snowflakes, 12, *14*, 24
Soda crystals, 41
Solids, 12
Solution, basic, 47–48
Solutions, 33, 47–48
Special crystals, 37

Sponge garden, 52
Sponges, 54, 57
Stalactites, *44*, 45
Stalagmites, 42, *44*, 45
Sugar crystals, 12, 19, 30, *31*
    experiments with, 33, 36, 39,
      40
Sulfur, 17
Super crystal gardens, 52–53
Supersaturated solutions, 33
Surprise garden, 53
Synthetic crystals, 27
Synthetic gems, 27

Table salt. *See* Salt
Transistors, 27

Utensils, 29

Walnut-shaped crystals, 38
Washing soda, 41, 42, 45
Water vapor, 24